101
MORE
TALKS
FOR
CHILDREN

MARIANNE J. SHAMPTON

101

MORE

TALKS

FOR

CHILDREN

Bookcraft
Salt Lake City, Utah

Library of Congress Catalog Card Number: 89-82697
ISBN 0-88494-729-7

Fifth Printing, 1997

Printed in the United States of America

To my parents
who taught me by their beautiful example

To my husband
who inspires and encourages me

To my five wonderful children
who are the joy of my life

Contents

Hints for Parents

When a child is going to give a talk it is important for him to choose a topic that is familiar to him or one that he is interested in. When the child chooses the topic himself he will be excited to give it, and it will be easier for him to remember it.

Many times a talk can be written around a single object. The child can tell in his own words what the object is and why it is important to him. He can tell what we can learn from the object or how it applies to a gospel theme. The object can be shown as the child talks and will serve as a focal point of attention for the audience. It will also help the child remember his talk.

Visual aids are helpful to both the audience and the speaker. Whenever possible, let the child draw pictures to go with his talk. This will help him understand his topic. It will also make it more interesting for the audience. If a child has prepared the talk and made visual aids, he will be more excited to share it and more willing to give the talk. At the end of some of the talks in this volume you will find a note that gives suggestions of possible visual aids your child might use.

In this book are several talks worded around an object or pictures, and these talks can serve as examples for your own ideas. They can also be personalized to fit the child's situation.

1

The Scriptures

Read the Scriptures

Our prophet has asked us to read the scriptures; he has told us how important the Book of Mormon is and that we should study it every day.

Why is it so important? The scriptures tell us about God and Jesus. They also tell us about the prophets and many prophecies. The scriptures tell us about the righteous and unrighteous people, and how living the commandments brought happiness and breaking the commandments brought sorrow and destruction. The scriptures tell us what we should do so we can return to live with Heavenly Father again.

3

When we read the Book of Mormon or Bible we should ask ourselves "How does this apply to me?" We need to make the scriptures a part of our lives.

When we read of King Benjamin teaching the people about service and love, we can learn how to serve others. When Jesus taught the people in Galilee about the beatitudes he was also teaching us. I hope we will read the scriptures every day and learn how to apply them in our lives.

Have Courage

We all like to hear stories about men who are brave and courageous. There are lots of movies and books about heroes and heroines. Even the scriptures tell us about such people. There were the two thousand stripling warriors who went to fight and not one was killed. They were brave; they did not fear, because of their faith.

There is the account of Shadrach, Meshach, and Abednego who were put in a burning, fiery furnace. They had courage. They knew that the Lord would protect them.

When Daniel was put in the lions' den he had courage. He knew the Lord would protect him.

Probably none of us here will be put into a fiery furnace or in a lions' den, but each of us needs to show courage and faith. The Lord tells us in Doctrine and Covenants 38:30 that "if ye are prepared ye shall not fear." And Doctrine and Covenants 68:6 reads: "Wherefore, be of good cheer, and do not fear, for I the Lord am with you."

The time may come when you will have to make a choice for good or evil. Sometimes it is hard to do what is right if your friends are trying to get you to do otherwise.

I hope we can all remember not to be afraid. We can have courage. We must have courage to say no to drugs, to drinking, and to smoking. We must say no to stealing, lying, and cheating on tests. If we decide now that we have courage, then we will not be afraid of what others might say. If we do this we will be as successful as any hero or heroine.

Never Too Young

I am only _____ years old, but I can still learn about the Book of Mormon. I know how Lehi brought his family to America.

I know how Moroni hid the golden plates in a hill. I know how Joseph Smith got the plates and translated them so we could read them.

We are never too little to learn about the Book of Mormon.

The Book of Mormon

When we read the Book of Mormon we learn about new people and places and things.

Nephi, Helaman, Captain Moroni, and Ammon are all men found in the Book of Mormon.

Zarahemla, the Waters of Mormon, and Jershon are all places found in the Book of Mormon.

The Liahona and the title of liberty are objects described in the Book of Mormon.

We can learn a lot by reading this book.

America, the Promised Land

I would like to tell you about several groups of people who were led across the oceans to this, the American continent, by the hand of the Lord.

The first group was the Jaredites. They came from the city of Babel. Because of their wickedness they eventually killed each other off.

The second group was Lehi and his family, who left Jerusalem. They became known as the Nephites and the Lamanites. The Nephites were all killed in war by the Lamanites, and the Lamanites today are known as Indians.

The third group to come to America was the Mulekites. They left Jerusalem about eleven years after Lehi. The Mulekites founded the great city of Zarahemla. They were found by Mosiah and merged with the Nephites.

About four hundred years ago Columbus discovered the American continent. Since that time many other people have come to that land.

The prophet Moroni said that America "is a choice land, and whatsoever nation shall possess it shall be free from bondage . . . if they will but serve the God of the land, who is Jesus Christ" (Ether 2:12). I hope we will remember this promise from the scriptures.

The Brother of Jared

Jared is a popular name. You might even go to school with someone named Jared. I would like to tell you about a man named Jared who lived many, many years ago. He lived before Christ was born. He lived before Lehi and Nephi.

Jared lived with his family in a city called Babel. The people of Babel decided to build a high tower. They worked very hard and the tower got higher and higher. They were trying to get to heaven with this tower. This upset Heavenly Father; the people were wicked, so he changed their language so they couldn't talk to each other. Because they could no longer communicate the work on the tower ended.

Jared had a brother who was very righteous. He prayed and asked the Lord not to change the language of his family and friends. The Lord answered his prayer. These people were called the Jaredites.

The Lord instructed them to build boats to cross the ocean. They built eight boats, but there were no lights inside to see by. After much thought, the brother of Jared got sixteen white stones and asked the Lord to touch the stones so they would glow and give off light. When Jesus touched the stones, the brother of Jared saw his finger. Because of his great faith, this man saw Jesus as a spirit. He looked like us. We are created in the image of God. The brother of Jared was one of the first men on earth to see Jesus, and it was because of his faith.

I hope we will all strive to have as strong a faith as the brother of Jared did. His name is not found in the Book of Mormon, but through modern-day revelation to the Prophet Joseph Smith we found out the real name of the brother of Jared. It was Mahonri Moriancumer.

Liahona

When Lehi and his family left Jerusalem they went into the wilderness. They needed a way to find out where they should go.

One day when Lehi came out of his tent he found a strange-looking object. It was round and had two spindles, or arrows, on it. It was made of brass and was called the Liahona.

The Liahona worked on the principles of faith and obedience. If the people were righteous the arrows pointed the way for them to go. Sometimes words appeared on the ball to give messages. However, if the people were not righteous, or if they didn't show faith and obedience, the Liahona didn't work.

This instrument was used throughout the Book of Mormon times. It was handed down from generation to generation.

Joseph Smith and the Three Witnesses to the Book of Mormon saw the Liahona when they saw the brass plates.

We do not have a Liahona, but we do have the Holy Ghost to lead and direct us. They work on the same principles. I hope we will keep the commandments and have the faith necessary for the Holy Ghost to guide our lives.

Nephi's Broken Bow

When Lehi and his family left Jerusalem they had to provide for themselves. Nephi and his brothers were in charge of getting food.

Nephi would take his fine steel bow and go with his brothers to hunt for wild animals. One day there was an accident; Nephi's bow broke. They were unable to get food. They went back to camp empty-handed. Laman and Lemuel were angry. Everyone was murmuring. Nephi felt very bad. He prayed to the Lord for help. He was told how to make a new bow. Nephi asked Lehi, his father, where to go to find food. The Liahona showed Nephi where to go.

We should all remember this story because we can learn from it. If we need help the Lord will provide it, if we ask him.

The Lord will help you if you are lost, or if you are studying for a test, or if you need help preparing a talk for Primary. If you need the Lord's help, ask him in prayer and have faith that he will help you, and he will. The Lord will help you just as he helped Nephi.

I hope we will all remember the lessons of Nephi's broken bow.

Lamanites

When we read the Book of Mormon we get acquainted with two groups of people, the Nephites and the Lamanites. Usually the Nephites were righteous and followed the Lord's commandments. The Lamanites were just the opposite; they were usually wicked and didn't obey.

However, there were some exceptions to this. Many Lamanites were righteous and loved the Lord.

For example, Samuel the Lamanite went to Zarahemla to tell the Nephite people to repent. They would not listen to him and they shot arrows at him as he stood atop the city wall. He was protected by the Lord and was not hurt.

The two thousand stripling warriors who followed Helaman into battle were another example of righteous Lamanites. Because of their great faith none of them was killed. They had been taught of faith by their righteous Lamanite mothers.

We should remember the examples of these Lamanites and try to pattern our lives after them.

Title of Liberty

I would like to tell you about Captain Moroni in the Book of Mormon. He was a very good man. He helped his people fight for their freedom and their families.

There was a wicked man named Amalickiah. He wanted to be their king and take away the people's freedoms.

People were choosing sides. Many went with Amalickiah. Captain Moroni knew he had to do something to motivate the righteous people to stand up against Amalickiah. Moroni tore off a piece of his coat. He wrote words on the coat. He attached it to a pole and used it as a flag. He called it the title of liberty. This was to help remind the people how precious their freedom was and how important it was for them to fight to save it. With Heavenly Father's help they won, and the wicked Amalickiah disappeared into the wilderness.

To help the people remember the title of liberty, a flag was put in every city. The words on the flags can help and inspire us today as much as they did the people in Book of Mormon times. They read: "In memory of our God, our religion, and freedom, and our peace, our wives, and our children" (Alma 46:12).

We should be thankful for all of these things.

Mormon

Near the end of the Book of Mormon we read about a man named Ammaron. He was a righteous man who listened carefully to the Lord and did as he was instructed to do. Ammaron was in charge of the gold plates. He did not want them to be destroyed, so he hid them.

Mormon, a ten-year-old boy, was very mature for his age and kept all of God's commandments.

Ammaron went to Mormon and told him where the plates were hidden. He told Mormon to remember the things he saw happening so when he was older he could add them to the plates.

Five years later, when Mormon was fifteen years old, Jesus Christ appeared to him and gave him further instructions.

Later on, Mormon got the plates from their hiding place and recorded the history. Mormon gave a few plates to his son, Moroni, and put the rest in the Hill Cumorah.

Mormon was killed in battle. In fact, all the Nephites were killed except Moroni. He was the last one to have the plates before Joseph Smith.

I like this story because it started out when Mormon was a young boy. I hope we can all remember his example and try to stay close to Heavenly Father by keeping his commandments.

2

Gospel Teachings

Baptism

Did you ever want to do something that someone else did? Well, I did. This was something special that I waited a long, long time for. I'll give you a hint. Maybe you can guess what it is. Joseph Smith did it. Jesus did it. My Primary teacher did it. Our bishop did it. Our Primary president did it too. I bet you know what it is. I'll tell you.

On _____ (*give date*) I was baptized a member of The Church of Jesus Christ of Latter-day Saints. This was important to me.

It was very important that Jesus was baptized too. In the Gospel of Matthew we are told that the heavens were opened and a voice from heaven came saying, "This is my beloved Son, in whom I am well pleased" (Matthew 3:17).

It is special when each one of us is baptized. If you have already been baptized, you should remember the covenants, or promises, you made. If you have not been baptized, you should study and pray and keep all the commandments so that when you turn eight years old you will be ready. We should all remember how important baptism is.

Bear One Another's Burdens

One of the songs in our hymnbook comes from Primary. It goes like this: "As I have loved you, love one another. This new commandment, love one another. By this shall men know ye are my disciples, if ye have love one to another." ("Love One Another," *Hymns,* no. 308.)

I know each of us wants to be counted as one of Jesus' disciples. In order to do this we must show our love for others by helping them. In Galatians 6:2 Paul said, "Bear ye one another's burdens, and so fulfil the law of Christ."

How do you bear someone's burdens? By helping them. If they are sad or lonely we can be their friend. If they are hungry we can share our food. If they are upset we can listen to them.

If we are friends to everyone we meet and try to help make their lives easier, then we are bearing their burdens. We are then worthy to be called disciples of Christ. I hope we will all be numbered as his friends, his disciples, his followers.

Blessings

The universe is governed by rules. There are laws that have to be followed. The earth, the planets, and the solar system were all formed within set guidelines.

The Lord also has chosen to set rules for himself to follow. For instance in Doctrine and Covenants 82:10 he says, "I, the Lord, am bound when ye do what I say; but when ye do not what I say, ye have no promise."

When we are given a commandment we are usually told the blessing that comes by obeying that law. For example, if we pay our tithing the windows of heaven will open with blessings for us. If we keep the Word of Wisdom we will run and not be weary; walk and not faint; and the destroying angel will pass over us.

The Lord wants to bless us. He wants to give us all he has, but he can't just give it to us. We must work and earn it by being obedient.

I hope we will keep the commandments so the Lord can give us all the blessings he has waiting for us.

Children May Need Help

Jesus loves little children. He cares about them and wants to help them.

When Jesus was on earth he took the children in his arms and blessed them.

After Jesus was resurrected he visited the American continent. He gathered the little ones together and blessed them. Angels came down from heaven and formed a circle around the children and administered to them.

God cares about the children today. He loves them and still wants to help them. Some children need help now. Sometimes they are afraid or hurt but don't know where to go for help.

Our prophet, President Benson, spoke about children in general conference on April 2, 1989. He told the children that there were angels who could administer to them and help them. They might not be seen but they would be close by. This should make us feel good inside to know we are not alone. If a child needs help he should talk to someone; it could be the bishop, his Primary teacher, a friend, or a parent. Many children have been helped because they decided to talk to someone.

I hope we will all remember that little children are loved and that the angels are there to help us if we will ask for that help.

Everyone Should Keep the Commandments

In Primary we sing the song "Keep the Commandments." Who is this talking to? Who is supposed to keep the commandments? Our moms and dads, our grandmothers and grandfathers, our aunts and uncles are all supposed to keep the commandments. And children, like us in Primary, should keep the commandments.

In the Book of Mormon when Alma was talking to his son, Helaman, he said, "O, remember, my son, and learn wisdom in thy youth; yea, learn in thy youth to keep the commandments of God" (Alma 37:35). We need to learn those commandments when we are young.

When we are in sacrament meeting listening to the speaker, or when we are in Primary listening to our teacher, or when we are at home listening to our parents in family night we should pay attention to what they are saying because they are telling us what the commandments are.

Whether we are 4, or 44, or 104, Heavenly Father wants us all to obey his commandments.

Faith

Faith is believing without seeing. It is trusting without proof.

In the scriptures we see many examples of people who had faith.

When the Israelites left Egypt to follow Moses to the promised land they came to the shores of the Red Sea. The waters were parted, and the people walked through them on dry land. This took faith.

When Lehi and his family built the ship and started sailing across the ocean to the unknown land, they showed their faith.

When we are afraid to do something, we should show we have faith and do it. We will never be alone because God will always be there to help us, even though we can't see him. We should trust in the Lord and show by our actions that we believe and have faith. It might be moving to a new place. It might be walking away from friends when bad words are being used. It might be giving a talk in church. Whatever it is we must do, we should not hold back or hesitate. We should go forward and do it. If we have faith we can do anything.

If you ask Heavenly Father, he will help your faith to grow. I hope we will all exercise our faith by using it every day.

Feed the Spirit

In Matthew 4:4 Jesus said, "Man shall not live by bread alone, but by every word that proceedeth out of the mouth of God."

Every day we make sure we eat and drink. This feeds our bodies.

We need to feed our spirits too. We can feed them by reading the scriptures. They are our spiritual food.

Just as we can't eat only one meal a week, we can't feed our spirits only once a week either. They need daily nourishment. That is why we should read every day. If you are too little to read, ask a brother or sister or your mom or dad to read to you today.

In John 5:39 Jesus was talking to the people and said, "Search the scriptures; for in them ye think ye have eternal life: and they are they which testify of me."

I hope you will start feeding your spirit daily.

Forgiveness

We hear a lot about repentance but not so much about forgiveness. But forgiveness is very important. We must be willing to forgive others if we want others to forgive us. This doesn't mean that we forgive once or twice. Jesus tells us that we should forgive seventy times seven. That is a lot of times. Jesus was really telling us that we should forgive others over and over again. We should always be forgiving.

If someone at school does something to hurt you, or someone in your neighborhood makes you feel bad, or if your little brother or sister breaks your favorite toy —you should forgive them.

None of us is perfect. We all make mistakes. When we do, we can repent, knowing Heavenly Father will forgive us. But how can we expect him to forgive us if we don't forgive others?

Another thing we need to remember is that when we forgive we should forget. That means we no longer remember it. We don't bring it up over and over again in conversations. If you truly forgive, you forget. It is over. It is just as if it never happened.

I hope we will all remember to be forgiving.

Heavenly Father's Love

Heavenly Father watches over everything and everyone on this earth.

He sees the butterfly emerging from the cocoon. He sees the honeybee fluttering from one flower to another. He sees the newborn colt struggle to stand on wobbly legs for the first time.

Heavenly Father sees the little girl timidly stepping into the baptismal font and taking hold of her daddy's hand. He sees the family at the airport as they wave goodbye to their grandparents leaving on a mission. He sees a five-year-old walking into school for the first time. He also hears a little child's prayer when he asks if the Book of Mormon is true.

Heavenly Father watches over all, because he loves all. I'm thankful for Heavenly Father's love.

I Love Jesus

I love Jesus. He is my friend. He is your friend too.

He helped many people when he was on earth. He healed people who were sick. He made the blind man see and the crippled man walk. He even used his priesthood power to bring his friends' brother, Lazarus, back to life after he had died. Jesus did all these things because he loved the people.

He will help us today. He tells us to call upon Heavenly Father in his name. I hope you love Jesus as I do. You can show you love him by keeping the commandments. I hope we will all do that. That would make Heavenly Father and Jesus happy.

Obedience

Doctrine and Covenants 58:6 reads: "Behold, verily I say unto you, for this cause I have sent you—that you might be obedient."

We must all learn how to obey. We should do this without questioning or hesitation. When your mom or dad asks you to do something, you should do it right then. Don't try to get out of it or ask why. We should listen and obey.

It is the same with our Heavenly Father. We should obey the commandments without asking why or trying to put it off until later.

Obedience is something we start learning from the time we are born. Babies and small children have to learn how to obey. The sooner we learn to obey the better off we are. The men and women in prison have not yet learned to obey.

I hope we will learn and be obedient to our rules at home and to the commandments our Heavenly Father has given us. It is important to obey.

Priesthood

I would like to talk to you about the priesthood. It was given to Joseph Smith and Oliver Cowdery by heavenly beings in 1829.

Sometimes we think the priesthood is only important to the boys. This is wrong. We all need the blessings that come from the priesthood. One important thing to remember is this—we can all help strengthen the priesthood in our homes.

As children we can help our older brothers and our dads to use their priesthood. We can remind them to do their home teaching. We can ask for a blessing when we are sick. You can ask your father for a father's blessing. In April and October when we have general conference there is a special session on Saturday night for the priesthood; we should remind our fathers of this session.

We should thank our Heavenly Father for the priesthood in our homes. We should ask him to help us honor that priesthood.

Sacrament

Every Sunday we go to church with our families. While we are there we take the sacrament. That is the most important thing we do on Sunday.

When we take the bread and water we should think about Jesus. That's all. We should sit quietly and think about Jesus, the stories he told, and the things he did.

I hope next Sunday when we take the sacrament we will all remember our brother, Jesus Christ.

Sacrifice

Sacrifice is a big word. It means to give up something or to go without.

We read about sacrifice in the scriptures. Abraham was asked to sacrifice his son Isaac. Jesus sacrificed his own life.

We also hear many stories about pioneers who sacrificed their homes and everything else they had. Some people even gave up or sacrificed their families to be members of the Church.

Little children need to learn to sacrifice too. Sometimes we give up our time to play. Sometimes we give up our pennies to the Primary Children's Medical Center. Sometimes we give food or clothes to help someone in need.

We should always be willing to sacrifice or give up something for someone else. This shows Heavenly Father that we love him. In Matthew 25:40 Jesus says, "Inasmuch as ye have done it unto one of the least of these my brethren, ye have done it unto me."

Testimony

On fast Sunday we listen to different members of the congregation stand up and bear their testimonies.

Do you have a testimony? Do you know how to get one?

In the Book of Mormon the prophet Alma tells the people of Zarahemla how to get a testimony. Alma tells the people they should have faith. They should want a testimony and believe they can get one. He tells them to fast and pray and ask for the Spirit to be with them.

It is the same for us. If we want a testimony we should ask Heavenly Father to help us. As we fast and pray and study, the Lord will help us gain one. Then we can stand and say we know the Church is true and that the President of the Church is a prophet of God today, just as Joseph Smith was a prophet in his day.

I hope we will all have the faith to gain a testimony. (*Bear you testimony.*)

Trust in the Lord

In Proverbs 3:5 we read: "Trust in the Lord with all thine heart; and lean not unto thine own understanding."

This is an important scripture and we should always remember it.

We are here on earth to learn and be taught. We do not always understand. Sometimes we may want to ask why? Why do I have to do that? Why can't I do it my way? Why can't I do it later?

We need to learn to obey and have faith. If we remember that our parents and our Heavenly Father want only the best for us, then we will remember they know what we should do and when we should do it. We are young and see only a small picture or view. They are older and see a larger picture. They see the whole view and know what we should do.

I hope we will listen to our earthly parents and to our Heavenly Father. I hope we will rely upon their knowledge and understanding to guide us back home again.

War in Heaven

I would like to tell you about a big war, a huge war, a gigantic war. This was probably the biggest war of all time. Even though we cannot remember it the scriptures tell us about this war. And we were all there—you, and me, and all our friends. We were all there to witness this war.

This war took place in heaven before we were born. Our Heavenly Father had presented a plan for us to come to earth to prove ourselves so we could return to him again. Two of our brothers, Jesus and Lucifer, wanted to help but in different ways. There was discussion and disagreement. Eventually Lucifer and one-third of the hosts of heaven were cast out because they rebelled. We know we were with the two-thirds who accepted the Father's plan and his choice of Jesus as Savior. We came to earth.

Today we are still fighting that battle. Lucifer, or the devil, is still trying to get us to follow him. He wants us to break the commandments. When we stay home from church or cheat on a test or tell a little white lie, we are losing the battle. In Doctrine and Covenants 10:5 the Lord gives Joseph Smith this counsel: "Pray always, that you may come off conqueror; yea, that you may conquer Satan, and that you may escape the hands of the servants of Satan that do uphold his work."

I hope we will remember to say our prayers; to keep the commandments; to choose the right way in our everyday life. If we do this, eventually we will win the war and be victorious over the devil. This war isn't a game; it is our eternal salvation. I hope and pray that we will all be counted on the Lord's side.

When to Pray

We hear a lot about prayer because it is very important. Prayer is the way we can talk to our Father in Heaven.

We should not pray just once or twice a day. We need to pray often. We should say both family prayers and individual prayers. We should pray when we get up in the morning and before we go to bed at night. We should pray when we have a decision to make. We can pray as we study and go to school. We should pray for courage to do what is right. We can pray anytime we need the Lord's help.

We should also remember to pray in order to give thanks to our Heavenly Father. When he answers our prayers we need to recognize that.

I hope we will all remember to pray.

3

The Articles of Faith

The Articles of Faith

The Articles of Faith tell what our church believes. John Wentworth, an editor for a newspaper in Chicago, wrote Joseph Smith a letter asking him what Mormons believed.

Joseph thought about the question. Then he wrote thirteen statements explaining our doctrine in a simple, easy-to-understand statement.

In Primary we are encouraged to memorize all thirteen articles of faith and to know what they mean. I have memorized some of them and would like to tell you the first one: "We believe in God, the Eternal Father, and in His Son, Jesus Christ, and in the Holy Ghost."

I hope to memorize all of them someday, and I hope each of you will want to memorize them too.

The Godhead

The first article of faith reads, "We believe in God, the Eternal Father, and in His Son, Jesus Christ, and in the Holy Ghost."

This teaching is very important to understand because it makes us different from many of the churches today. They believe that all three are the same person.

We believe they are three separate, individual persons. The first is Heavenly Father, the second is Jesus, the third is the Holy Ghost. They are three individuals who work together with one purpose.

When Joseph Smith was in the Sacred Grove he saw two persons: God, the Father, and Jesus, His Son. This is important doctrine and something we should remember.

I am thankful for all three members of the Godhead.

Second Article of Faith

The second article of faith says, "We believe that men will be punished for their own sins, and not for Adam's transgression."

This means we are not punished for what our parents or our friends do wrong. We are only punished for what we do wrong. Our Heavenly Father is just and fair.

If you touch a fire you get burned, but you learn not to touch fire. It is the same way with the commandments. If we break a commandment or do wrong we are punishing ourselves, but we learn not to do it again. It is better to learn to obey the commandments because we want to please the Lord rather than having to learn obedience by being punished.

I'm glad that we are only punished for what we do wrong and not for what others do wrong. I hope we can learn to do what's right more of the time so that we show the Lord we love him.

Called of God

The fifth article of faith reads: "We believe that a man must be called of God, by prophecy, and by the laying on of hands by those who are in authority, to preach the Gospel and administer in the ordinances thereof."

This article of faith is very important. Not just anyone can be a prophet. Heavenly Father picks out who the prophet will be. Then that man must be set apart for that calling.

It is the same with our bishop. Heavenly Father chooses the man to be bishop, then he is set apart by priesthood leaders who lay their hands on his head and bless him.

It is the same with other callings. We believe Heavenly Father tells the bishop who to give Church jobs to and then the bishop sets them apart for those jobs.

We should be thankful for this process. Because men and women are called of God we know they are always the right ones for those callings.

The Bible and the Book of Mormon

"We believe the Bible to be the word of God as far as it is translated correctly; we also believe the Book of Mormon to be the word of God." This is the eighth article of faith.

The Bible was written by many different prophets whose writings were collected and handed down from generation to generation. In this process, however, many "plain and precious things" were lost from their writings. The Bible is still a wonderful book, and we love it, but it is not as complete as it once was. A few hundred years ago the Bible was translated into different languages by men who loved the Lord and wanted everyone to be able to read that book.

The Book of Mormon was different. It was especially written on golden plates, mainly by the prophet Mormon, to come forth by the power of God in our time. An angel gave these plates to Joseph Smith to translate, and the Holy Ghost told Joseph Smith what was written on them. This book was translated correctly with the Lord's help.

Both the Bible and the Book of Mormon tell us about Jesus Christ. We should read both of these books.

Revelation

"We believe all that God has revealed, all that He does now reveal, and we believe that He will yet reveal many great and important things pertaining to the Kingdom of God." This is the ninth article of faith.

We know that through our prophets the Lord has told us, or revealed to us, his will. We know that when the President of the Church tells us to do something, he is speaking for the Lord.

We believe the Lord will continue to direct us in the future the same way he did in the past. In other words, he is our director—past, present, and future. The Lord did guide us yesterday, he does guide us today, and he will continue to guide us tomorrow and for all tomorrows to come.

We should listen to the voice of the prophet because he speaks for God. I am thankful for revelation.

Eleventh Article of Faith

"We claim the privilege of worshiping Almighty God according to the dictates of our own conscience, and allow all men the same privilege, let them worship how, where, or what they may." This is the eleventh article of faith, and it is an important one.

We are blessed that we live in a country where we can worship the way we want to. We can be Latter-day Saints because we want to.

However, we should let other people do the same. If your friend does not want to become a member of our church, that is okay. He can still be your friend and you should respect his religion. You should never make fun of his beliefs. You should love him for what he is, a child of God. We should never put down someone else's religion.

4

Families

Families in the Scriptures

Throughout the scriptures we read about families. The first family was Adam and Eve. We learn about two of their sons, Cain and Abel. We read about Noah and his family being saved in the ark from the Flood. We read about Lehi taking his family out of Jerusalem and over to the promised land. We learn of his sons Nephi, Laman, Lemuel, and Sam. We read about Alma and his son along with Mosiah and his four sons.

The families changed, the situations changed, but one thing remained the same. If the family worked together there was peace and happiness. If the family fought and disagreed there was contention and unhappiness.

It is the same for us today. Families must work together. If we work together there is harmony. If we work against each other there are problems.

I hope we can learn from the families in the scriptures and make our own family better.

My Family

All families are special, but I think mine is the best. We all love each other and have fun together. When I say my prayers I thank Heavenly Father for my family.

(*Show a picture of your family that you have made or a photograph of them.*) This is my family. (*Point out each member of your family and tell who they are.*)

We should tell our families that we love them. We should all work together so we can be a family forever.

Mothers

I know someone who has so many jobs that she is always busy. She is a teacher, a nurse, and a beautician. She cooks, sews, and sings. She is the first one up in the morning and the last one to crawl into bed at night. She is my best friend—she is my mother.

I am thankful that Heavenly Father sent me into our family because my mom is the best mom for me.

I hope we will all show our mothers how much we love them by doing the things they ask us to do.

Fathers

In June we celebrate Father's Day. We are proud of our fathers and they deserve a special day to honor them.

There are many kinds of fathers. First we think of our earthly fathers as our dads. They provide food and clothes and shelter for our families. They work hard at their jobs. They spend time playing with us. They set a good example for us.

Another father is our Heavenly Father—he is the father of our spirits. He loves us and cares for us. He watches us carefully and listens to our prayers. By answering those prayers he helps us in our earthly life.

We have still another father. He is the father of our ward. We call him the bishop. He loves us too. He worries about us; he prays for us; he spends many, many hours doing ward business to help the families in the ward.

I hope we will show all our fathers how much we love them.

Brothers/Sisters

I love my family.
I love my brothers.
I love my sisters.

It is fun to have brothers or sisters. They can play games with you. They can read to you. They can fix a broken toy. They can help you get ready for church. They can be with you if you are afraid.

I am thankful for my brothers and sisters.

Note: Use the words *brothers* and/or *sisters* as they apply. Your child could show a picture of his or her brothers or sisters.

Love at Home

In church we sing a song that starts out, "There is beauty all around when there's love at home" ("Love at Home," *Hymns*, no. 294).

Homes come in different sizes and colors. Some are large; some are small. Some are made of wood; some are made of brick. Some homes are built in the mountain tops while some are built on the beach by the ocean. But this is not important. It doesn't matter where your home is built or what materials were used to build it.

Home is where you live. And that's what counts. You are the one that makes the difference.

Love and harmony between all family members are important. The fact that you are all there together under one roof is important.

The beauty of your home isn't the grass and flowers on the outside in your yard. The beauty comes from within those walls as the family members help and support each other, as they sing and pray together. In this way our homes can all be alike; they can all radiate the love of the gospel from within.

I hope all our homes will be beautiful with love.

My Best Week

The first day of the week is Monday. That is when we have family home evening. It is a great way to start the week.

During the rest of the week we read the scriptures and have family prayer. We try to do what Jesus would have us do. The last day of the week is Sunday. It is our day of rest. It is the day to go to church and remember Jesus and Heavenly Father. It is the right way to end the week.

If we start and end the week on a spiritual note and stay close to the Lord during the rest of the week, then we will have a better week. If we do this we can make our homes a little bit of heaven on earth.

Missionary Farewell

In Matthew 28:19 Jesus commands his disciples: "Go ye therefore, and teach all nations, baptizing them in the name of the Father, and of the Son, and of the Holy Ghost."

That is exactly what my brother is going to do. He was called to go on a mission to _____. (*Write in the place.*) He accepted that call happily.

I know he will make a good missionary because he made a good brother. He was always there to help me and I know he will be there to help the Lord. He set a good example for our family so I know he will set a good example for the converts. Whenever he makes up his mind to do something he does it. Nothing can stand in his way. I know this determination will see him through a lot of difficult times. I know also that he loves the Lord because he told me he does. I know he will do a good job and that the Lord will be as proud of him as I am.

I am going to write him letters and pray for him so he'll know I haven't forgotten him.

If you have a brother or sister who is thinking about going on a mission, you should encourage him or her. We should remember the missionaries who are serving the Lord all over the world. We should give them our love and prayers.

Grandparents on a Mission

Missionaries come in all colors and all sizes. Some of you may have a brother or sister who is on a mission. Some of you may have a mom or dad who served a mission.

I'd like to tell you about my missionaries. That's right, missionaries. I have more than one. I have two—my grandmother and my grandfather. They were called to serve in the _____ Mission.

Sometimes I miss them, especially on holidays or my birthday. But it is fun when we get letters from them. They tell us about the people they are teaching the gospel to. Sometimes they even teach children. I know they make good missionaries, and that is why Heavenly Father called them to go. I know he will watch over them even though they are far away.

I can pray for them. I can write them a letter or draw them a picture. I can even send them a Book of Mormon with my picture and testimony in it so they can give the book to someone they are teaching. I guess that makes me a missionary too.

If your grandparents are thinking about going on a mission, let them know you'll be very proud of them and that you'll give them your support.

I'm thankful for missionaries and grandparents.

Note: The child could show a picture of his grandparents.

Genealogy

Families are important. When we think about families we usually think of our mom and dad, our brothers and sisters, and our grandmothers and grandfathers. But we should not stop there. A family goes on and on and on. Great-grandparents, great-great-grandparents, uncles, aunts, and cousins all make up our extended family.

The scriptures tell us the hearts of the fathers shall turn to their children and the hearts of the children turn to their fathers. This means we should be concerned for our relatives; we should do genealogy. As children we should encourage our parents to go to the temple. We should write in our journals. We should help our moms make a family history. We can help with family reunions. We should ask our parents to tell us about our relatives who have died.

I hope we will turn our hearts, our love, and our interest to our relatives, dead or alive, young or old, so we can help with genealogy.

5

All About Me

I Used to Live in Heaven

I used to live in heaven with Heavenly Father and Jesus. When I left there I came to earth to live. While I am here I must show Heavenly Father I can keep all of his commandments and do what is right. When I'm eight I will be baptized. When I get married it will be in the temple. If I do these things I will be able to live with Heavenly Father and Jesus again someday.

I hope we will all try to do what is right so we can return and live with God again.

51

I Can Learn

When I was born I couldn't do anything but cry and sleep. I had to learn how to crawl; then how to walk. I had to learn to say a word or two at a time: *Mom, Daddy, drink.* I learned how to run and skip and jump. When I was old enough to go to school I learned how to read and write, how to add and subtract, how to think and reason. When I started going to Primary I started learning new songs and meeting new people. I learned to be reverent in Heavenly Father's house. I know I have a lot more to learn —we all do—but if we take it one step at a time we can do it.

I hope we will all sit quietly in our classes and learn from our teachers. The Lord instructed us in Doctrine and Covenants 88:77: "And I give unto you a commandment that you shall teach one another the doctrine of the kingdom." I hope we will all enjoy learning.

My Body

Heavenly Father gave me my body and I should take good care of it.

I should eat good food like apples and carrots.

I should brush my teeth and see a dentist.

I should exercise, like riding my bike.

I should go to bed early.

I'm thankful for my body; I hope you are too. We should all take good care of our bodies.

52

New in Primary

My name is _____. I am three years old. I just started coming to Primary. I am a Sunbeam. I like Primary.

My favorite song is _____. My favorite scripture story is _____.

We should all get to know each other because we are all brothers and sisters in the Church.

I Am a Star

I am four years old.

I am in the Star class. I like being a Star.

At night when I look out the window and see all the stars in the sky it reminds me of my Primary lesson.

Because I am a Star I should shine bright for everyone to see. I should be the best Star I can be.

Read Out of the Best Books

I am _____ years old. I am going to school and learning how to write and read. It is fun. I like to read. First I learned the alphabet; then I learned individual words; then I read sentences. Soon I'll read books.

We are told in the scriptures to read good books. This counsel is in Doctrine and Covenants 88:118: "Seek ye out of the best books words of wisdom." We are taught by our parents and teachers to watch good movies, not bad ones. It is the same for books.

Good books teach us things. Examples of good books are the Bible, the Book of Mormon, and the *Friend*. The library has a lot of good books for us to read. There are many LDS authors who write just for children so we can have good books. We should let our parents help us pick out books.

President Benson has talked about reading. He suggested that children could start their own file of stories and pictures and things.

I hope we will try to read more books that help us learn and grow.

Numbers

I have been learning my numbers: 1-2-3-4-5-6-7-8. Sometimes the numbers remind me of things I have learned in Primary.

1. Jesus said, "Love one another."
2. At least two of every kind of animal went on the ark with Noah.
3. When you are three you get to go to Primary.
4. Four books make up our standard works: the Bible, the Book of Mormon, the Doctrine and Covenants, and the Pearl of Great Price.
5. Jesus fed five thousand people with five loaves of bread.
6. The Bible says the earth was made in six days.
7. The seventh day is Sunday—a day of rest.
8. I can be baptized when I turn eight.

I love to learn my numbers, and I like to come to Primary and learn about the gospel.

Note: The child could hold up each number as it is mentioned.

Important Twos

My little brother (*or sister*) is learning about numbers. I started to think about how many things come in twos.

Missionaries preach in twos.

Parents come in twos—one mom and one dad.

Noah took at least two of every animal on the ark.

I go to two meetings on Sunday—Primary and sacrament meeting.

Two books of scripture are witnesses of Jesus Christ—the Bible and the Book of Mormon.

A bishop has two counselors to help him.

We always have two choices—right or wrong, good or bad.

Joseph Smith saw two people in the First Vision—Jesus and Heavenly Father.

The sacrament consists of two parts—bread and water.

My Favorite Words

I would like to tell you about some of my favorite words.

Monday—I like Monday because that is the name of the day we have family night.

Hurry—I like the word *hurry* because that is what I tell mom and dad to do after dinner so we can start family night.

Treat—I like this word because we end our family night with a treat each Monday night.

Happy—This is what my family is when we have family home evening. The more we have it the happier we are.

My very favorite words of all are these: *Family Home Evening*—I love family night. I hope you do too.

If I Were . . .

Do you like to pretend? I do. Sometimes I pretend to be someone else.

If I were a flower I would share my sweet fragrance with everyone who walked by the garden.

If I were a bird I would sing a joyful song.

If I were a bee I would make the sweetest honey.

If I were a tree I would stand up straight and tall and point my leaves toward heaven.

But I am not really any of those things. I am a child of God. I will be the best child I can be.

I hope you will be your best too.

Note: The child could draw pictures of a flower, a bird, a bee, and a tree.

If I Could Go Back in Time

If I could go back in time, I would like to meet a lot of people.

I would like to meet Brigham Young and be with him when he entered the Salt Lake Valley and said, "This is the place."

I would like to meet Joseph Smith and help him hide the golden plates. Maybe we would hide them under my bed.

I would like to meet Joseph of Egypt and see his coat of many colors.

I would like to meet Moses and watch him part the Red Sea.

I know I can't go back in time and meet these people, but I can read about them in the scriptures and in Church history.

Maybe I will be here when Jesus comes again and will be able to meet him then. I need to live righteously and keep the commandments so that when I do see him I will be worthy and can live with him again.

Moving—A New Place To Be

Hi, my name is _____. I am _____ years old. We just moved here from _____.

Sometimes it is hard to move. It is hard to meet new friends and go to a new school.

I am sure it was hard for Nephi and his brothers to leave Jerusalem with their father, Lehi, and head for the wilderness. It was difficult for them to build a boat and sail across the ocean. They not only left their town of Jerusalem but also their country, and they set sail on a strange ocean not knowing where they were going. When they finally landed and got off their boat there were no houses. There were no neighbors to welcome them.

I guess I was better off than Nephi. Reading their story in the Book of Mormon helped me adjust when we moved. I was glad our neighbors welcomed us and that I could come here to Primary. I hope I can get to know all of you.

I Love Primary

I like to come to Primary. It makes me feel good inside when I see my teacher smile at me. I like the songs we sing. But I think the best part of Primary is when we go to class and my teacher tells us stories about Jesus and Heavenly Father. I like to hear the story about when Jesus took the little children and blessed them.

I hope you like Primary too. If you know someone who is not coming to Primary you should invite them to come.

I Am a Child of God

I am a child of God, and because I am I have a great responsibility. You do not have to be an adult to do great things. I would like to remind you of three young people we read about in the scriptures.

Jesus grew up and became strong. When he was only twelve years old he was separated from his family. After searching for him they found him teaching in the temple. When questioned as to what he was doing he replied he was about his Father's business.

We have all heard the story about David and Goliath. One point in that story is often forgotten. David was the youngest one in his family. He was the "little brother," yet he was the one who slew Goliath and saved the people of Palestine from being slaves.

The last one I would like to tell you about is Joseph Smith. He, a boy of fourteen, not an adult, inquired of the Lord and received a vision. It was through the faith and prayers of this young boy that the gospel was restored.

The young people of our church are important. Each one of us is important both to the Church and to our family. You are a child of God. Each one of you can help your family grow stronger in the Church.

There are little ways you can encourage your family. Remind them to read the scriptures daily. Remind them to hold family home evening. Remind them to pray. Remind them to fast.

I hope we will all remember that we are sons or daughters of God. We are his children. Each one of us is important. I hope we will all try to do our part.

The Friend

I have a friend who is very special to me. We share good times together. This friend has a lot of ideas and a lot of different activities we can share. Do you know who my friend is? I'll tell you. (*Hold up the* Friend *magazine.*) This is my friend.

I love to get it in the mail every month. It has stories, poems, and pictures. It has riddles and puzzles. It has a calendar for that month. Sometimes it has a new song in it. I enjoy every single page.

I like this special friend. I'm glad they make a magazine especially for kids. It teaches me about the gospel and helps my testimony grow. If you have this friend, read it and share it with others.

Note: Use the *Friend* as a visual aid.

6

Living in this World

Anger

There are many scriptures that talk about anger.

Proverbs 15:1 reads: "A soft answer turneth away wrath but grievous words stir up anger."

Also, in Proverbs 29:22 we read: "An angry man stirreth up strife, and a furious man aboundeth in transgression."

It is wrong for us to be angry. We should control our thoughts; that way, if we start to get upset, we can calm ourselves down before we get really angry. Singing a song, counting to ten, or reciting a scripture are all different ways to help control our anger.

The scriptures also tell us that the devil is the father of contention and that he tries to get us angry with each other. We don't want to be helping Satan, so we shouldn't fight or get mad.

I hope we will all try harder to keep our tempers under control.

Attitude

One of the first songs we learn in Primary starts, "Jesus wants me for a sunbeam to shine for him each day."

We should try to start each new day like a sunbeam. When we get up out of bed in the morning we should think about being happy. We should put smiles on our faces before we leave the bedroom.

If we think happy thoughts we will be happy and we can radiate that happiness and sunshine to all we meet. As we read in Proverbs 17:22, "A merry heart doeth good like a medicine."

I hope we will all try to radiate sunshine everywhere we go, all day long.

Fear

Paul tells us in 2 Timothy 1:7: "For God hath not given us the spirit of fear; but of power, and of love, and of a sound mind."

Heavenly Father does not want us to have fear. We should not be afraid of anyone or anything. If we are afraid we should pray to him and he will help us and turn our fear into courage.

If you are lost or alone; if it is dark and you cannot see; if you have to make a courageous decision, Heavenly Father can take your fear away and replace it with the knowledge that he is with you. You and the Lord can do anything.

I hope we will learn to turn our fear into courage.

Goals

It is now the beginning of a brand new year. People everywhere are talking about setting New Year's resolutions. That means they are setting goals for the coming year.

We are all encouraged to set goals. In the older Primary classes the boys and girls set goals in specific areas. When these goals are accomplished they earn an award.

It is good to set goals so we can improve ourselves. It makes people feel good about themselves when they accomplish their goals. Various people have different goals, and we all need to improve in different areas.

Some possible goals might be to say individual prayers every morning and every night, do homework without being reminded, and read the scriptures daily. These are just a few possibilities. I hope we will all set goals for ourselves to work on.

Gossip

There is a game called "Gossip" that is fun to play. The person who starts the game whispers a secret to the person sitting next to him. That person whispers what he thought he heard to the person next to him. And so the game proceeds, each passing on the secret he hears. The game ends when the last person tells out loud what he heard. The fun comes because usually the secret changes as it is passed from one person to another. This game of gossip is funny. But in the real world gossip isn't funny. Gossip can hurt people.

We should never listen to gossip. Ecclesiastes 3:7 says there is "a time to keep silence, and a time to speak." It is easy to know the difference. If you are saying something to build someone up, it is the time to speak. If you are about to say something that would put someone down, it is the time to be silent.

I hope we will all remember not to gossip and try instead to make our conversations good and uplifting.

Health

Nowadays it is popular to be healthy. Everywhere we go we see people running, or jogging, or walking down the street. People join health clubs and do aerobics. We are all reminded during the Olympics how important it is to keep our bodies healthy.

We need to exercise daily; eat good food; get enough sleep and rest.

We see No Smoking signs in public places.

We see bumper stickers that read "say no to drugs."

We hear reminders not to drink and drive.

The public is just now discovering what we, as Mormons, have known for years — that some things are good for our bodies and others are not. The Word of Wisdom was given to us to help us have healthy, strong bodies so we could live longer and enjoy life more.

The scriptures tell us that man is that he might have joy. I hope we can all keep the Word of Wisdom and keep our bodies as a temple, so we will know more joy and happiness.

Making the Right Choice

President Spencer W. Kimball said: "Life gives to all the choice. . . . You can be common, ordinary, dull, colorless; or you can . . . be clean, vibrant, progressive, useful, colorful." (*The Miracle of Forgiveness,* p. 235.)

The choice is up to us. We can be whatever we want to be. But we must decide now. Each choice we make determines part of what we are becoming.

If we want to be a concert pianist, a prima ballerina, or an Olympic gold medalist, we must make that choice now and practice every day. If we want to be a missionary we should make the choice now to study and gain a testimony.

Each of us can become like God and have all that he has. The choices we make now also affect our eternal goals. I hope we realize how important our choices are and that we will make the right choice every time.

Mind Your Manners

We should remember to mind our manners and to be polite.

We should always say please and thank you. We should share and not be stingy. We should never talk with our mouths full of food or interrupt someone who is talking. We should always wait our turn and never push into line.

These are things our parents have told us a hundred times, but we need to be reminded. It is important for us to have good manners and set a good example for others to follow.

Mistakes

We all make mistakes. But mistakes can be fixed. If you tear a paper you can fix it with tape. If you tear a button off your shirt you can mend it with a needle and thread.

If we break one of the commandments we can fix that too. It's called repentance. Repentance is the way we fix mistakes in our lives. When we do something wrong we need to repent. First we say we are sorry. Next we try to right the wrong. We promise never to do it again. The Lord then forgives us. This is made possible by the Savior's sacrifice for our sins.

I'm glad Heavenly Father taught us about repentance. I hope we will all try to do what's right, but when we don't I hope we will remember to repent.

Music

In Primary we learn lots of new songs. Some are fast and some are slow. Some are sung loudly and some are sung very quietly. Some of them are reverent, while some of them are sung just for fun. All of them are special.

We sing songs when we are in church, but there are other times when we can sing. If we are sad we can sing to make us happy. If we think a bad word or a bad thought, we should sing a song to put a good thought in its place. If we are angry we can sing to help calm us down. If we kneel down to say our prayers at night, we can quietly sing a song to put us in a reverent mood to get us ready to pray.

I am thankful we can sing. I like learning new songs too. I hope we will all join in for singing time in Primary.

Opposition

In 2 Nephi 2:11 Lehi teaches his son Jacob: "For it must needs be, that there is an opposition in all things." Life was not meant to be easy. Life is a test, and part of that test is seeing how we react to opposition.

Everything has an opposite—black and white, happy and sad, sick and well, hot and cold, good and bad. We must experience both so we can appreciate the good things.

It's hard to go up the stairs, but it's fun to go down a hill. It's hard to brush our teeth, but it's good to hear the dentist say "no cavities."

The next time you find yourself doing something that is hard for you, remember that Heavenly Father will always be there to help and support you.

Peace

Everywhere we look we see people fighting. The newspapers and television show pictures of war. All this fighting is bad. Heavenly Father doesn't want us to fight with each other.

We cannot change the world, but we can do something. We can bring peace to a small part of the world. We can have peace in our homes.

There is much we can do as children. We can stop arguing. We can get along with our brothers and sisters. We can be peacemakers in our neighborhoods. We can help the kids at school to get along with each other. When we say our prayers, we should ask Heavenly Father for more peace.

We will never have peace in all the world until Jesus comes again, but we can have peace around us if we do our part. Jesus said, "Blessed are the peacemakers" (Matthew 5:9).

Peacemaker

Jesus taught: "Blessed are the peacemakers: for they shall be called the children of God" (Matthew 5:9). This same scripture is also found in the Book of Mormon. This must be very important if Jesus told the people on both continents the same thing.

What do peacemakers do? They help solve problems. They try to make everyone else happy. They never argue or fight. They give instead of get. They are easy to get along with. They settle arguments. They never insist on getting their own way.

We can be peacemakers at home with our families and at school with our friends. If we try to be peacemakers we will have more friends and be happy. We will have the Lord's Spirit with us.

I hope we will all try to be peacemakers.

Prepare

In Doctrine and Covenants 38:30 the Lord made the promise: "If ye are prepared ye shall not fear." Do you know what it means to prepare?

Prepare means to put together or to get ready beforehand. If we prepare or get things ready we won't need to worry about being ready.

For example, if you do your homework you are prepared for school. If you practice on the piano then you are ready for a recital. If you have a bath and wash your hair on Saturday then you are ready or prepared for Sunday.

We should always think ahead.

If we keep the commandments and do all that we are asked to do, then we will be prepared for when Jesus comes again. I hope we will try to be prepared in all areas of our lives.

Service

A lot of the scriptures talk about the importance of doing service for others. The scriptures tell us that if we love God we can show that love by serving others.

When King Benjamin was talking to the Nephites from his high tower he said, "When ye are in the service of your fellow beings ye are only in the service of your God" (Mosiah 2:17).

We should look around our homes and our neighborhoods to see whom we could serve. Lots of people need help. We could shovel someone's sidewalk when it snows. We could rake leaves in the fall. We could walk someone's dog or take a younger child to the park. We could visit someone who is sick or too old to get outside. We can bake for a neighbor or make a card for the sick.

There are lots of ways even a child can be of service. I hope we will all look for ways to serve.

Doctrine and Covenants 42:29 reads: "If thou lovest me thou shalt serve me and keep all my commandments." Let's show the Lord how very much we love him.

Sharing

My mommy and daddy told me that I should be nice and always share with others.

There are many things I can share:

I can share my smile.

I can share my toys.

I can share my books.

I can share my testimony.

I can share a cookie with my best friend.

I like to share. I hope we all will remember to share. It makes Heavenly Father and Jesus happy when they see us share.

Note: The child could draw pictures of the things he/she could share.

Smiles

What is a smile? Someone once said, "A smile is a curved line that sets things straight."

Someone else said, "A smile is the light in the window of your face that tells people your heart is at home."

In Primary we sing a song called "Smiles." "If you chance to meet a frown do not let it stay. Quickly turn it upside down and smile that frown away."

If more people would smile there would be less arguing. Everyone would be happier.

I hope you will remember to smile more often. When you get up in the morning, the first thing you should put on is a smile. If you share that smile with everyone you meet, your day will be filled with sunshine.

Solution to Boredom

"I'm bored!" Have you ever said that to your mom? You just can't think of anything to do. Well, I have a solution for you.

Stop thinking of yourself and think of someone else. It could be a friend you like to play with. It could be an old man who lives at the end of your street. It could be the little boy who broke his leg. It could be your grandma or grandpa. It could be anyone. The important thing is that you think about someone else and do something for them.

You should soon be busy with thoughts of them, either helping them or doing something for them. If you want it to be really fun, do it in secret—surprise them.

The scriptures tell us to think about others and forget ourselves. It can be fun, and it's never boring.

Testimony Meeting

The first Sunday of every month is fast Sunday and people bear their testimonies in church.

Mom and Dad bear their testimonies. Grandma and Grandpa bear their testimonies. Sometimes teenagers bear their testimonies. Sometimes Primary children stand and share their testimonies too, but it is really scary to stand up in front of all the adults.

I do have a testimony, and I would like to share it with you today. (*Bear your testimony.*)

This Beautiful World

We have all heard the story about when the earth was created in six days. I am so glad that it was made to be a beautiful earth. I love the green trees that blow in the wind. I love the yellow daffodils and tulips that bloom in the spring. I love the blue of the lakes and strcams. Thc tall mountains and lush valleys make the earth more beautiful.

All the colors and variety in nature make our land so lovely to look at. I am thankful for this earth.

I hope when we go outside we will take time to appreciate all we see.

Note: The child could hold up a colored piece of paper as each color is mentioned.

Thou Shalt Not Steal

When Moses was on Mount Sinai, he was given the Ten Commandments. I would like to talk about number eight, "Thou shalt not steal."

We might think to ourselves that we would never steal. We would never be a thief. However, I wonder if we steal without realizing it.

When we are noisy in church, we take away the reverence.

When we are late for a meeting we take someone else's time.

When we litter we take away from the world's beauty.

If we use someone else's idea without giving them credit we are stealing.

I hope we will be honest in all we do and say. I hope we remember to keep all of the commandments.

Time

How many hours are there in a day? Most people would answer there are twenty-four hours in a day. I know I have twenty-four hours in my day.

How many times do we hear the excuse "I couldn't do it because there wasn't enough time?"

The world turns around and around. The sun rises and sets. The clock goes on and on ticking away every second. Whether we are asleep or awake, working or playing, time goes on.

If we want to accomplish something we must be aware of time. Some people do a lot in one day while others waste it. We should make good use of all our time.

I hope we will all make our time count so that we will accomplish something every day and make good use of the time our Heavenly Father has given us.

We Are What We Think

Proverbs 23:7 reads: "For as he thinketh in his heart, so is he."

This means we are what we think. If we think happy thoughts, we are happy. If we think sad thoughts, we are sad. If we think good thoughts we do good deeds. That is why what we think about is so important.

If we think we can accomplish a task, we can. If we think we will fail, we will. If we think we can reach the celestial kingdom and live with Heavenly Father again, we will.

I hope we will concentrate on good thoughts, and if we occasionally have a bad thought we should immediately replace it with a good one.

Who Needs Me?

Who needs me? Every day we should look around us for someone we can help. It may be a little girl who fell down and skinned her knee, or someone at school who dropped his book and papers. It may be the new kid at school who hasn't made any friends yet, or the little boy the big kids are teasing.

Heavenly Father wants us to help other people. We should do this every chance we get. We should look for people to help at school, at home, and in our neighborhood. I hope we will ask ourselves, "Who needs me today?"

Withstanding Temptation

In Mark 14:38 Jesus said to Peter, "Watch ye and pray, lest ye enter into temptation. The spirit truly is ready, but the flesh is weak."

Every day we are tempted to do wrong. Every day we must choose between good and evil. Heavenly Father knows this is hard and sometimes very, very difficult. But he will help us if we ask for his help.

When we pray we can ask God to help us withstand temptation. He can help us be strong and make the right choice.

I hope we will always remember to ask Heavenly Father for his help.

Work

In Genesis 3:19 the Lord says, "In the sweat of thy face shalt thou eat bread." In this scripture the Lord was talking to Adam after he had been driven out of the Garden of Eden.

In the world, Adam and Eve had to learn to work hard just to exist. They had to plant and cultivate the soil to grow fruits and vegetables.

We also need to learn to work because each one of us has work to do. There are a few things to remember about work:

1. Always do your very best.
2. Finish what you start.
3. Do your work without being reminded.
4. Do your work without complaining.

Whether it's making your bed, washing the dishes, taking out the garbage, or doing your homework, remember those four rules.

Work is necessary. We all must do it. I hope we will try to have a better attitude when it comes to work. We should thank Heavenly Father that we are healthy enough to be able to work.

7

Special People,
Special Times

Blessings in a Year

When I look at the calendar it reminds me of the many things I am thankful for. Each month seems to have a special meaning:

January— I am thankful for a new year to set goals in.

February— I am thankful for my family that I love.

March— I am thankful for the wind so I can fly kites with my friends.

April— I am thankful for Jesus' resurrection.

May— I am thankful for my mother.

June— I am thankful for my father too.

July— I am thankful for my country and the pioneers.

August— I am thankful for our garden.

September—I am thankful for autumn leaves.

October— I am thankful for general conference so I can listen to our prophet on TV.

November—I am glad we have a day to be thankful. I like Thanksgiving.

December— I am thankful that Jesus was born.

I hope we will all remember to be thankful for every day of every month of the year.

Note: The child could show a picture for each month.

Fast Sunday

Today is the first Sunday of the month. When we woke up this morning we didn't fix a bowl of cereal, or cook some eggs, or make pancakes. We didn't have a drink of orange juice or milk. That's because it is fast Sunday.

Heavenly Father wants us to skip two meals and then give the money we saved to fast offerings. The deacons go to every house in the ward to collect the money. They give it to the bishop to buy food for the people who don't have anything to eat.

Even though I am small I can go without breakfast. It won't hurt me, and it makes me feel good inside to know I am helping the poor. I know Heavenly Father is proud of all of us when we fast. I hope we can remember to fast next fast Sunday.

General Conference

Twice a year, once in April and once in October, the members of The Church of Jesus Christ of Latter-day Saints gather together in a special meeting. These meetings are held in Salt Lake City, Utah. These meetings are called general conference.

Our prophet and President of the Church and the other General Authorities meet in the Tabernacle. We sustain the General Authorities and Presidency of our church. We can listen to the Tabernacle Choir sing praises to the Lord. We can see and hear the prophet tell us what the Lord wants us to do. This meeting is on television and radio, and because of satellites this meeting can be seen all over the world.

General conference is special. We should try to remember what is talked about. Sometimes it helps to write down each speaker's name and what he talks about. Younger children can draw a picture to remind them of general conference.

I hope we will all remember to listen to general conference and then try to do what our leaders tell us to do.

Love

This is the month for love, because Valentine's Day is celebrated in February. Most people think of a romantic love. But today I would like to talk about a different kind of love.

In Matthew 22:36–39 a man asked Jesus, "Master, which is the great commandment in the law?" Jesus said to him, "Thou shalt love the Lord thy God with all thy heart, and with all thy soul, and with all thy mind. This is the first and great commandment. And the second is like unto it, Thou shalt love thy neighbour as thyself."

This means we should love God. We should love our neighbors. We should also love ourselves.

Did you send yourself a valentine? No, I'm sure none of us did. But we should love ourselves. We should be proud of our names and proud of our accomplishments. We should feel good about ourselves and remember that each of us is a child of God.

When we truly love ourselves we are more able to love other people and to love God.

March Seventeenth

On March 17 we celebrate St. Patrick's Day. Everyone wears something green. Green, green, everywhere we look.

I thought about this and all the beautiful green things God created. Green grass, green leaves, green caterpillars, green apples, green eyes, green peas, and green parakeets.

Green is a very pretty color. I am thankful for all the green things the Lord made.

Note: The child could draw a picture for each green thing he talks about.

Easter

When we celebrate Easter we think about when Christ was crucified. We remember he suffered for all our sins. He died for us. He was then resurrected. Some churches use the cross as a symbol to remember Christ. We do not. We think beyond his death to his resurrection.

Jesus lives! Because he lives we will live again.

If any of you have had a loved one die, you know how much you miss them. But it does help to know that you will see that person again.

I hope we will all remember why we celebrate Easter and show how grateful we are by keeping the commandments.

Easter Symbols

Sometimes we use symbols to help us remember things. At Easter time many people use eggs, flowers, new baby chicks, and bunnies as symbols for this holiday.

Easter means resurrection or new birth. An egg that hatches a baby chick is like new birth. Flowers blooming after winter is like new birth. Baby bunnies are born in the spring. All these things should remind us of Christ's resurrection.

As we look around and see the symbols of Easter I hope we will all picture Jesus in our minds and remember he was resurrected and that he lives.

June, July, August

June, July, August. Summer is almost over. I love summer because it is so much fun. We plant gardens, go on vacations, have family reunions, and get a break from school. We eat lots of watermelon, chicken, and corn on the cob. We have parades and fireworks as we celebrate our country's birthday. It's a great time of year.

I'm thankful Heavenly Father made the different seasons of the year and I'm especially thankful for my blessings this summer.

Constitution of the United States

In July we celebrate the founding of the United States of America. On July the Fourth we became a free nation.

Did you know that our Heavenly Father helped those men write the Constitution? Doctrine and Covenants 101:80 reads: "And for this purpose have I established the Constitution of this land, by the hands of wise men whom I raised up unto this very purpose, and redeemed the land by the shedding of blood."

Heavenly Father brought the Jaredites to America. He brought Lehi and his people to America. The Book of Mormon tells the history of these people. Heavenly Father guided Columbus to this land. He wants America to be strong. He helped establish our government, but it is up to us to keep it great and free.

You and I are important. We should remind our parents to vote. We should stand straight and tall and proudly say our Pledge of Allegiance. We should set a good example. We should remind our parents to display our country's flag on holidays. We should pray for our country's leaders that they will make the right decisions.

As children we can make a difference. I hope we will inspire others to be good citizens.

Pioneers

Have you ever thought what it would be like to be a pioneer?

Pioneer children did not have nice warm beds or warm houses. They slept on blankets in a wooden wagon or on the ground. Pioneer children didn't go to school all day. Instead, they spent their time from sunup to sundown walking and walking and walking alongside the wagon. Pioneer children didn't watch TV; they sang songs around the campfire. Pioneer children didn't have a beautiful chapel to go to Primary in. They didn't even have Primary.

Pioneer children had a life very different from ours. But one thing we have in common is the gospel. They were members of The Church of Jesus Christ of Latter-day Saints and so are we. I'm thankful they followed Brigham Young and settled in Utah so our church could grow in the tops of the mountains.

Thanksgiving

I love this time of year. We are all so busy. There is so much to do in the fall. We go to school; we harvest the garden; we have fun with trick or treats on Halloween; we look forward to Christmas.

Wait a minute, let's back up. Christmas doesn't come after Halloween. What about November?

November is a special month and we shouldn't pass it by. We should take time for Thanksgiving. We should stop and think about all we have to be thankful for. We should remember the pilgrims and how America came to be settled. We should be thankful for the freedom of religion we have.

I hope as we indulge ourselves with turkey and pumpkin pie we will take time to ponder our blessings and be grateful for all we have.

Note: You could end this talk by bearing your testimony and telling what you are grateful for.

Teachers and Leaders

Heavenly Father has given many people to lead and guide us. We should know who these people are.

Our Primary teachers and Primary president care for us very much. Our bishop, home teachers, parents, and brothers and sisters are also there to teach us.

These people are here to teach us, to show us what to do, and to help us when we need them. Heavenly Father gave us these special people because he loves us. We should be thankful for all those people who help us find our way back to Heavenly Father.

My Primary Teacher

I like my Primary teacher. She is so nice. She is here every Sunday. She smiles at me and that makes me happy. She teaches me about Jesus and Heavenly Father. When I see her during the week she always says hello to me. This makes me feel special.

When I am reverent, and listen to my teacher, it makes Heavenly Father happy. I hope we will all listen to our Primary teachers in Primary today.

My Home Teachers

I would like to tell you about two friends of mine; they are friends of my family too. They visit us once a month and sometimes more. They bring us a lesson that teaches us more about the gospel. If we need a blessing or extra help my mom and dad can ask them to help us. I bet some of you know who I am talking about — my home teachers.

We all have home teachers. We should make them feel welcome when they come to visit us. We should show them we want to be their friends. We should listen to what they say because it is important.

I am thankful for my home teachers and I hope we can all show them how much they mean to us.